THE FRENCH ROOM

THE
FRENCH
ROOM

SIMPLE FRENCH STYLE FOR YOUR HOME

ELIZABETH WILHIDE

WITH PHOTOGRAPHS FROM
LA MAISON DE MARIE CLAIRE

INTRODUCTION BY
TERENCE CONRAN

ARCH CAPE PRESS
New York

First published in 1989 by
Conran Octopus Limited
37 Shelton Street
London WC2H 9HN

This 1990 edition published by Arch Cape Press,
distributed by Outlet Book Company, Inc.,
a Random House Company, 225 Park Avenue South, New York,
New York 10003.

Senior Editor Polly Powell
Art Editor Karen Bowen
Picture Research Nadine Bazar
Production Shane Lask
Editorial Assistant Henrietta Gill

ISBN 0 – 517 – 051761
87654321
Printed in Hong Kong

Typeset by Hunters Armley Ltd., Leeds and London

CONTENTS

CONTRASTS

HARMONY

INTRODUCTION

The chances are that if you look closely at a French room, you may well be able to identify an Italian light, an English print or an Indian rug. But the way in which these elements are selected, arranged and used will betray something of that characteristic *élan* which the French always display when it comes to the visual world.

A good deal of French culture has to do with what one might call the external manifestations of life — architecture, fashion, art, sculpture, cuisine — all of which to some extent take place outside the home. For ordinary French people it was not until after World War II that interest in the domestic interior really took off, when entertaining became more home-based and it suddenly mattered what kind of impression everyday surroundings were making on guests and visitors.

La Maison de Marie Claire, from which most of the photographs in this book have been taken, has for 20 years been something of a style-setter for a new generation, consistently providing a framework which makes it easy to relate, for example, art to interiors, or fashion to interiors. The French have a profound understanding of clothes and this developed sense of style has been translated effortlessly to interior decoration. In the same way, the restaurant, for so long a hub of French life, has also had an important influence on the domestic scene, so much so that it is often difficult to tell the difference between a restaurant kitchen or eating area and a kitchen or dining room in a private house.

This book identifies the three most important strands of contemporary French style: the pure or natural approach, reflecting a positive delight in the varied effects of light; the ultra-modern or 'contrast' approach, which has its origins in the high style of the 1920s and 1930s; and the traditional approach which synthesizes eclectic elements with an instinctive but increasingly sophisticated flair.

When it comes to decoration, the French do have certain natural advantages. The raw materials they build on are often excellent, especially in older houses. There is the scale and proportion of the rooms, the quality of detailing — mouldings, catches, handles — and the superb features such as fireplaces, wonderfully sculptural bathroom fittings, herringbone flooring and large shuttered windows. Typical of Parisian interiors are sumptuous finishes, created by painting, rubbing down and filling walls over and over again. And, as far as furnishing is concerned, France is bordered by the vital cultures of Germany, Italy and Spain, which promotes a free flow of influence.

The essence of French style, however, applies to everyone. The attitude of selection, arrangement and economy, the appreciation of light, proportion and detail, and above all the sheer enjoyment of everyday things is really what good design is all about.

Terence Conran.

PURITY

*Minimal or sculptural,
the pure look is a decorating strategy
which makes use of plain fabrics,
natural materials and ordinary finishes
to create calm, deceptively simple rooms.
There is no better way to appreciate
the qualities of light and space.*

One of the most popular French styles to emerge in recent years is epitomized by the pale, perfect room, devoid of clutter, colour and pattern, yet classically serene and light. Pure white space is an ideal, even an extreme, but it is surprisingly easy to achieve, as well as being economical, comfortable and un-demanding.

Depending on how you interpret the style, it can be either spare and sculptural — emphasizing the proportions of a space, the solid geometry of planes and angles — or it can be soft, rather fragile, a subtle interplay of textures, and faintly nostalgic. Closely related is the natural look, 'pure' in the sense of 'real', understated and undecorated.

Both aspects of the style originated in the early decades of the twentieth century. In the 1920s, the decorator and wife of Somerset Maugham, Syrie Maugham, overturned decorating convention by creating the 'all-white' room, a look which became immediately fashionable and widely copied in both Europe and North America. Synonymous with sophistication and luxury, it was the very opposite of turn-of-the-century interiors, with their rich patterns, clutter and heavy lines. At about the same time, the design philosophies of the Bauhaus and of the Modern Movement's leading exponent, Le Corbusier, promoted the functional interior, with emphasis on the quality of the space rather than what was put in it — twentieth-century asceticism.

But there are also more traditional sources of inspiration. Sunwashed tropical and Mediterranean houses, for example, are bleached on the outside, refreshingly white and cool on the inside, with terraces shaded by split cane — this pure look is a natural and practical response to life in a hot climate. Conversely, it is also a good way of making the most of light in northern countries, where daylight is limited and precious. The large windows, pale colours and blond wood of classic Scandinavian interiors display just such a solution.

What all of these approaches have in common is that they demand restraint — the ability to live without clutter. And, because dirty marks and the signs of everyday wear and tear are particularly noticeable, there is also the need to be fairly scrupulous about cleaning and maintenance. There are many advantages. Cosmetically, small rooms will look bigger and lighter; awkward or conflicting features will be given consistency and unity. And the look can often be very inexpensive to achieve.

Above left The pure look promotes a sense of calm and contemplation, an antidote to the pressures of modern life. *Above right* A composition in white: painted wood, marble, glazed pottery, frosted glass and amaryllis. *Opposite* Natural light is an important element.

Nature can be a powerful source of inspiration, even for a style which appears to be the height of sophistication and restraint. There is an abundance of white flowers, each variety with its own distinct shade of white — greeny-white lilies, roses tinged with pink, pure white lily-of-the valley. The strong, clear light of the Mediterranean, dappled on terraces shaded by vines or cane, or filtered by shutters, is another potent influence, as is the traditional response to it — whitewashed houses with thick walls painted to reflect the light and to keep the interiors cool. Purity can also mean simplicity, in the sense of plain white crockery, natural pale wood or bleached calico; in fact, the style often works best using unpretentious materials and finishes. For inspiration, the purity style looks to objects for their shape, texture and pattern; the tiniest details are sufficient in such a sparse environment.

Above The delicacy of this fine window, with its oriental-inspired painted decoration
of flowers and birds, is reflected in the subtle modulation of textures —
the tasselled lace shawl draped over the sofa, ribbed carpeting and the
display of dried gypsophila.

On the face of it, the pure look is all about coordination — a fairly straightforward and rigorous coordination of white or natural, neutral shades. But it is not as simple as it sounds. First of all, white comes in different 'colours', subtle but nevertheless noticeable variations of tone and tint. Secondly, although colour may be coordinated, textural contrast can also be an important element, preventing the final effect from looking monotonous, insipid or monastic.

Creating an all-white room can be the simplest decorating task, *or* it can be rather more demanding. White is the perfect coverup, a good way of making awkward existing features recede and different surfaces, such as brick, woodwork and plaster, look consistent and harmonious. But if the aim is to create the type of purity which relies on spare, sculptural form, white can be very revealing. Minor defects will look more like major eyesores: in this case, both structure and surfaces must be sound and perfectly finished. This involves paying particular attention to the plasterwork: ensure that rough plaster is replaced, cracks are filled and any unevenness is smoothed out before the application of either matt or semi-gloss paint.

Above left Exposed beams, an open staircase and coir matting bring the warmth of natural tones to an otherwise all-white scheme. **Above right** All-white decoration can be demanding. In this immaculate dining room, tones match and finishes are perfect.

exploit the difference. As long as there are enough variations of tone, the whites will blend together. Different whites do not 'clash', but a yellowish white will look grubby and discoloured next to a blue-white. Varying texture, tint and tone will make the effect less noticeable: using shades such as off-white, cream, ivory and tinted pastel whites, as well as natural colours, such as stone or mushroom, extends the palette further.

White and near-whites can be combined effectively with sisal, coir, wicker and pale woods, without detracting from the pure look. The light, bleached-out tones of these natural materials read as 'no' colour, although they do contribute a sense of depth and warmth to an otherwise all-white decorative scheme.

PATTERN AND TEXTURE

For the purposes of this particular style, pattern and texture are one and the same thing. Obviously, a look which relies on the absence of strong colour excludes all but the most delicate tone-on-tone prints. However, there are other ways to introduce rhythm, vitality and depth to such a scheme.

THE PALETTE

Pure white is an elusive shade. In commercial paint ranges, for example, white commonly includes a tint of blue to produce the 'brilliance' promoted by manufacturers. Other whites are intrinsically warm, with underlying yellow tints; some whites 'yellow' naturally with age. White also varies according to the paint finish (matt, eggshell or gloss) and according to the context in which it is used — for example, the type of underlying surface used as the base, the other shades close to it, and the existing conditions of natural light.

The same variables apply to fabric, floor coverings, tiles, wallpaper and other materials. The reflectiveness of the surface, its textural properties and the scale of application result in a surprisingly wide range of tones from warm to cool, as well as sparkling to mellow.

What this all means is that if you decide to adopt a strictly coordinated approach, you may have to spend time searching for the right vinyl tiles to match the paintwork, for example, or to limit your choice of furnishing fabric to one particular type to keep visual continuity. But it is equally possible to

Above Grey walls give depth to an otherwise rigorously white room. The perfectly finished painted floor is an important element.

One way is to exploit the natural pattern or texture of fabrics, materials and finishes. The formal grid of ceramic tiling, the dappled effect of lace panels, the coarse irregularity of slub weaves, the filmy transparency of muslin — textural qualities are thrown into relief because there is little else to distract the eye.

As with colour, you can put like with like. Venetian blinds, ceramic or marble tiles, smooth white walls, glass and chrome, for example, are all elements that would keep the look hard-edged and formal. Alternatively, matt paintwork, gauze muslin or lace at the windows, armchairs draped with plain cotton and white cord carpeting would create an enveloping sense of comfort and softness. For a forthright rustic or natural look, painted brickwork could be combined with coir matting, linen loose covers and wicker furniture.

Contrast, however, is usually more effective than matching textures too precisely. A room in which all the surfaces are hard can be relentless and severe; similarly, one which is entirely soft may be rather insipid. Judicious use of contrasts — hard with soft, smooth with rough — helps to maintain a sense of liveliness and variety.

Above Indian cotton drapery mellows the light; the floor covering is coir matting.
Left Walls stippled with a sandy colour to resemble stonework.

The best way to achieve pure white walls and ceilings is to paint them, using the base coat stocked by most trade suppliers. Designed to be applied as an undercoat or as a foundation for tinted finishes, this type of paint is a truer white than popular commercial varieties.

An alternative solution, although rather more laborious, is to use distemper. Although it was once standard household paint, distemper is no longer in production, but the ingredients are still available and can be mixed up at home. However, it is in-compatible with modern paints: surfaces must be stripped before the application of distemper, and a distempered wall must also be stripped before it can be covered with standard paint. But the particular advantage of distemper, which can make all the effort worthwhile, is its unique chalky finish.

Professional decorators have long specialized in creating 'aged' white finishes, using a range of tints to achieve a quality of depth and character. White has a tendency to discolour, becoming yellower, or warmer, with time. In a room where a new coat of white paint might look too fresh and bright, small amounts of artists' colours, such as raw umber and sienna, can be mixed into a plain white base to simulate the gentle patina of age.

In recent years manufacturers have extended their range of whites and near-whites to include pale, luminous pastels: whites with tints of blue, yellow, green or pink. Clearer and more subtle than conventional pastels, these tinted whites supply just a hint of colour without detracting from the purity of an all-white scheme. A pinkish-white, for example, can be warmer than a plainer white in a dark, north facing room.

Another variable to consider is the texture of the finish: matt, midsheen or eggshell, or gloss. Matt, the most popular choice for walls, is soft and dull; midsheen, often favoured by professional deco-rators, is silky and glowing; gloss is highly reflective and sparkling. Midsheen or gloss can increase light and a sense of space in awkward corners, for example, under a dark stairway or beneath a deep gallery.

Not every wall consists of an expanse of smooth plaster. There may be exposed brickwork or beams, wood panelling, tiling or architectural details such as cornices, picture rails and dados. In most cases it is easy enough to paint or whitewash these different surfaces so that they blend in with the rest of the wall but retain their textural interest. Panelling can also be bleached or limed to lighten the tone of the wood.

Above For a bright attic room, panelled walls and ceiling painted white make the
most of available light. Windows have been left bare. The sofa upholstery
was originally sea-blue; to fit into the scheme, it has been covered
with a length of light fabric.

Top Pale sky-blue walls make a refreshing background for a shower room. The floor
is tiled in plain white ceramic tiles. ***Above*** Bathroom walls, tiled to
three-quarter height, are supremely practical, utilitarian and crisp-looking,
and also reflect all the available light.

In a simply decorated, pure white space, the floor will receive more attention then usual. Real purists will insist on white floors, carefully matched in tone to other white surfaces. Equally acceptable are natural floor coverings such as coir or sisal, pale polished wood and carpeting in neutral shades — all of which are light enough to preserve the unity of the look.

The options for hard floor coverings include various types of tile and sheet flooring, most of which are generally available in pure white. Sheet linoleum is a good choice for a seamless white surface and is very easy to maintain. Linoleum tiles also make a practical plain background, although the joins will always be visible. For a cool, slightly formal Mediterranean look, ceramic tiles are the best option, whereas marble tiles are the ultimate in luxury and sophistication.

Existing wooden floors can be lightened in a number of ways to fit in with an all-white scheme. Floorboards can be painted white using a durable finish such as yacht paint. Alternatively, they can be bleached, whitewashed or gessoed and subsequently sealed with a clear varnish or a light polish with wax. All these treatments will result in a pale, glowing surface where the grain of the wood

Above *Marblized floorboards match the countertop and splashback.*
Right *White painted floorboards, varnished to a glossy shine.*

is still visible. When choosing new wooden flooring, opt for types which are naturally light, such as maple, beech, ash or birch, rather than the rich tones of teak, iroko, redwood or mahogany.

Carpeting is available in a range of light, natural tones, from off-white to stone, beige and pale mushroom. Berber carpet, which is flecked throughout, has a sense of depth; natural white cord can be luxurious in areas such as bedrooms, where the floor receives less wear.

Rugs, such as cotton dhurries, which can be easily removed and cleaned, can help to protect a pale carpet from the effects of heavy traffic in areas such as hallways and landings.

Hardwearing, easy to maintain and understated, coir, sisal or seagrass matting can be laid wall to wall like carpet or bound in widths to make a temporary covering. Matting adds textural interest and provides the perfect foil for pale rugs. In addition to pale natural colours, there are sophisticated versions with light greys or creams, woven in a variety of patterns. Because matting is now available with latex backing, dust is no longer a serious problem and most types are less likely to fray around the edges.

***Above** A study in textures: the hard stone floor is softened by a deep pile rug, which also serves to define a conversation area.*

Whatever daylight a room receives will be emphasized and enhanced by all-white or pale decoration. The way windows are treated is all important. For example, a 'sense' of light can be increased by exploiting the light-filtering quality of semi-transparent fabrics such as muslin and lace, or the ability of shutters, blinds and louvres to create interesting patterns of light and shade.

If the design of a window is worthy of attention, the simplest and most effective strategy is not to cover it at all. As long as privacy is not of prime importance and the views are good, features such as beautifully detailed French windows, elegant sashes, or graceful arched or rounded windows are often interesting enough to be left well alone. This type of bare simplicity is naturally compatible with the pure look. Absence of colour in the interior means that the eye is drawn to what the window reveals, bringing the outside world indoors. For a slightly softer look, which provides a degree of privacy but does not block out too much light, windows can be framed or draped with lightweight, semi-transparent fabrics. Lace is one of the best ways of filtering light. Its delicate patterning and inherent charm always look fresh and romantic.

Lace is best treated very simply and either threaded onto a fine rod or wire, hung close to the glass in panels, or loosely gathered and suspended by ties. A similar effect can be achieved by using gauzy muslin, voile or fine net.

Windows which need to be screened more effectively can be covered in curtains or blinds made of heavier material. Again, because colour is absent, the emphasis will be on texture and form. Canvas or wool curtains hang in sculptural folds which can be very effective in a modern room, whereas glazed cotton curtains or plain cotton roller blinds look crisp and neat. Fabrics with a forthright texture, such as linen and slub weave varieties, suit the tailored style of Roman blinds. Another option is to line plain cotton curtains in a pastel shade — when the light shines through, the room will be suffused with a pale tint of colour.

Many types of blinds and shutters filter light in an interesting way; some, such as Venetian blinds, offer the opportunity to control it. White Venetian blinds are a good choice for a hard-edged purity; paper and cane blinds give a more natural look, whereas shutters and louvres painted white have a strongly Mediterranean flavour.

Above left White cotton drapery with a discreet stripe trails on the floor.
Above centre Tall windows screened by panels of plain fabric. Above right
Sail-like roller blinds for angled rooflights. Opposite White Venetian
blinds look modern and elegant.

The quality of lighting is always important, but especially in a pure interior. Obviously, obtrusive fittings can spoil the effect; more crucially, lighting which is harsh, glaring or unsympathetic in tone can make all-white decoration look stark, uncomfortable or just dingy.

In a pure room, the 'colour' of an artificial light source is more evident. Compared to natural light, which is judged to be 'white', artificial light sources vary in their ability to maintain tonal values and colour relationships, differences which can be important if a decorative scheme is based on careful combinations of pale shades. The most common domestic light source is tungsten, a warm, flattering light which has a marked yellow cast. Tungsten is a sympathetic choice for a scheme relying on warmer whites or pastels, or for enhancing pale natural colours, but it may be too yellow for pristine white rooms. Fluorescent light, including the low-voltage variety, has a greenish tinge which makes it uncomfortable and stark in a pure setting. Halogen, however, is a sparkling white light, quite close to

natural light, and very effective at creating a sense of drama or for preserving distinctions between closely related schemes.

The angle and intensity of light is another important factor. Pure interiors which are decorated in a 'soft' way, with fabric, matting, or other combinations of textures, need correspondingly soft, diffused lighting, from low-level table lamps, for example, or dimmer-controlled wall lights or pendants. A 'harder' look can be achieved by using directional spotlights, downlights or uplighters for crisp definition.

It is not difficult to coordinate light fittings with pure schemes. Most of the standard styles are available in white, off-white, pale grey or cream, including plaster wall-mounted uplighters, track spotlights and ceramic table lamps. Chrome is also a common finish for functional types of light fitting, a material which is perfectly at home in a pure setting. And since white is a standard colour for lighting accessories, such as switches and sockets, there is no need to spoil the effect with unsightly outlets.

Above Uplighting concealed behind a deep cornice gives a look of elegance and refinement. A mirrored wall reflects the scenic view. **Opposite** Tungsten, the most common domestic light source, is essentially warm in tone, giving this all-white decor a distinctly yellow glow.

Once the basic decorating is complete, pure style can then be interpreted in a number of different ways, depending on the type of furniture you choose and how you arrange it.

Because colour is subdued, the emphasis as far as furniture is concerned will be on shape and form. In other words, since you cannot rely on creating a sense of liveliness with sharp accents of colour, you will have to pay special attention to the way different shapes complement each other. In a minimal room, each piece of furniture will be displayed like an object in space; crisp, defined shapes are often the most effective in this type of environment. In a softer, more upholstered interior, draping sofas and armchairs helps to blur the outlines so that hard edges disappear. But, in each case, it is often a good idea to counterpoint the prevailing mood by adding something different. In a minimal space, for example, a solid armchair, perhaps with loose covers, can prevent the effect from looking too spindly; a clean-lined table in an upholstered room will help to set off the flowing lines of fabric.

Whichever approach you choose, the pure look is always summery and airy: there is a strong sense of the outdoors. Positioning mirrors to reflect views and light, and arranging furniture to make the most of windows, will emphasize this connection. The window, rather than the fireplace, is the focal point of the room.

*Left Simple loose covers. **Above** The crisp lines of tailored upholstery. **Opposite** The height of femininity — a bed draped in white cotton.*

The pure look is one of the easiest and most economical ways of putting a room together. Almost any type of furniture can be adapted to fit in with an all-white scheme, from fine antiques to humble café chairs. The unity of strict coordination means that old and new will blend comfortably and even quite disparate pieces will look as if they belong together. It is not a style which demands that you have grand furniture: white paint or new covers can provide an instant facelift for a junk shop find.

Garden furniture is very much at home in a pure interior because of its association with the outdoors. Simple metal park chairs painted white, Lloyd Loom basket chairs, canvas deck-chairs and practically anything in cane or wickerwork all work well. Simple in style, cheap, readily available and easy to adapt with paint or upholstery, many of these pieces of furniture have inherent textural interest.

Wooden furniture is not incompatible with pure style. In the 1920s and 1930s, when pure white rooms were the epitome of luxury and so-phistication, wooden finishes were 'pickled' or limed — artificially lightened in order to blend in with the decor. Many pieces can be painted white or bleached, but furniture made of woods which are naturally light in tone, such as ash or beech, can add a touch of warmth without looking too dominant.

Modern designs in materials such as chrome, aluminium, laminate and formica have a crisp, utility look which suits the minimal approach. Glass-topped tables or metal trestles supporting white laminate tops maintain the sense of space in a pared-down setting.

Top left and **Above** *Garden furniture is sympathetic to the pure look.* **Top right** *The warm tone of stripped wood can be a useful visual anchor.*
Opposite *Traditional upholstered furniture, pale wood and cream festoon blinds emphasize the fine plasterwork mouldings in this period room.*

Many pieces of furniture can be readily transformed with new upholstery, loose covers or drapery so that they blend in with a pure scheme. Fabric will add an important textural dimension, but there is a problem with maintenance, which varies depending on the style of covering you choose. Drapery or loose covers can be removed easily and washed or cleaned; tailored upholstery should be avoided in areas which are likely to be subjected to heavy wear and should be treated with a proprietary fabric spray to protect it against dirt.

'Close' covering can be used to reveal the shape and line of classic styles such as Empire *recamier* couches, upright square or oval-backed chairs and modern sofas. There is a range of suitably sturdy furnishing fabrics, including linen or linen union, light tweeds and wools and various cotton blends, but it is hard to better the simplicity of natural white calico.

Removable loose covers range from precisely tailored coverings that fit the piece so snugly that it looks almost upholstered to lengths of fabric simply draped and tucked in place. The neat appearance of the tailored style of loose covering can be accentuated by trimming with piping and finishing the skirt with box pleats. Heavier material which resists crumpling is best. By contrast, covers which are designed to fit less exactly can be made in standard cotton — the casual, unfinished look is part of the charm.

And, at the most extreme, loose covering can consist of just draping a sofa or armchair with a swathe of fabric, allowing the material to fall in folds at the corners and overflow onto the floor. This

Above left A fabric-lined room can look both luxurious and intimate. Above right A canopy of fine net looks supremely romantic.

vaguely mysterious and romantic look — evocative of grand empty rooms shrouded in dustsheets — could not be easier or cheaper to achieve. It is important to be generous with the fabric you use, but simple, plain cotton sheeting is just as effective as a more expensive material.

Fabric is also a good coverup for those tables which otherwise would not fit into a pure scheme. Occasional or bedside tables can be dressed with full skirted cloths which fall to the floor; kitchen or dining tables can be set with traditional white linen or damask, heavy lace or even white oilcloth — depending on the mood you wish to create. Trimming cloths with heavy cotton fringing, edging, zigzags or scalloping adds vitality and a sense of movement as well as providing detail to supplement the textural elements.

Bed drapery is one of the most enjoyable and theatrical ways of using fabric in pure interiors. A drift of filmy net suspended from a rod, a plain wooden or metal framework hung with lined cotton curtains or a canopy shrouded in loops of fine muslin all immediately create a sense of romance and femininity which can be perpetuated in the choice of bedcover and bedlinen. Candlewick bedspreads, frilled cotton valances, embroidered linen, pillowcases trimmed with delicate lace or broderie anglaise — there is great potential for subtle textural contrast. If you prefer a simpler style, choose fitted bedcovers in heavy fabrics such as linen union or rep, trimmed with piping, or alternatively a plain quilt stitched in a gridded pattern with a plain, padded bedhead.

Above An over-sized sofa with white loose covers makes an effective background for pale striped cushions.
Left Chairs draped in white sheeting.

Top A white bedroom is the perfect retreat — peaceful, soft, light and airy. **Above** Floor-to-ceiling shelving stores books and records away from the main living area.

A pure interior is an antidote to the stresses and distractions of modern life, but even one room decorated in this way can be a peaceful oasis in the middle of a busy household. The style has different benefits and makes different demands depending on how and where it is applied; an entire house or apartment will require much more planning than a single room.

The most important aspect to consider is storage. Inevitably, even with the most careful attention to detail, there will be various household necessities — clothes, books, records — which will not conform to the pure look. A wall of bookshelves, for example, which would comfortably blend into a decorated room in warm colours and patterns, becomes a vivid focal point in a white space. For most people, this is a perfectly acceptable intrusion. Strict purists or minimalists, however, go to great lengths to make sure nothing spoils the purity and simplicity of the decoration. Building cupboards behind the scenes to take everyday clutter is one solution; devotees have even been known to cover books in white cartridge paper so that all colour is banished. But even if you are fairly easy-going, the success of the look does depend on being rigorous about what is on display and there is a need for more storage than usual. Obviously, if only one room is decorated in this way, things which do not fit in can be put elsewhere.

The pure style is a celebration of light and space, but there are more specific associations, depending on the function of the room. In living rooms, white or natural decoration promotes a simple enjoyment of texture, a feeling of relaxation and calm and a sense of luxury. In dining areas, pure style makes a fresh setting for food. White kitchens and bathrooms suggest practicality and efficiency; white bedrooms are the ultimate in relaxing tranquillity.

Above Country-style purity. *Left* A richly decorative setting for a festive occasion, full of frills, flowers and lace. Even the wine is white.

Above *The elegant, faintly 1930s atmosphere of this living room relies on the clean
lines of the upholstered sofas and chairs and the modern severity of
floor-to-ceiling Venetian blinds, symmetrical arrangement and careful details such as
the octagonal occasional table and the chrome drinks trolley. The style
recalls the first period of popularity for the all-white look and the chic, sophisticated
drawing rooms of that time which provided the stylish backdrop
for their elegant occupants.*

Above In a completely different interpretation of the pure look, a sense of restrained decoration directs attention firmly to the beautiful architectural quality of the room — the magnificent stone fireplace, the mellow quarry-tiled floor, and the fine details of the door and shutter panelling. Simply by draping the sofas in white sheeting and restricting any additional decorative touch to an arrangement of white and pastel flowers, the result is memorable and evocative. The room provides a cool retreat from the outside heat.

Right Pared-down modernity in a vast, open-plan space. *Below* A laminate table and bentwood chairs under a stark skylight. The black-and-white photographs on the walls pursue the graphic theme. *Centre* A marble-topped pine table lends a homely touch to a sleek modern kitchen. *Opposite: Above left* The busy grid of ceramic tiling and the shelves of glassware and crockery make a sympathetic marriage of traditional and modern. *Above right* A picnic table set up for impromptu outdoor meals. *Below right* Quarry tiles set off by fresh white paintwork and country-style furniture.

Right A concrete platform in this cool, severe bedroom has an inset bath. Rough plaster, broken pottery and the classical urn suggest an air of antiquity. *Below* A shop display case which has been painted white makes unusual storage. Pure white tiling and paintwork looks gleaming and fresh. *Opposite* Unbleached muslin draped over a plain framework turns a bed into a room within a room. The cream shawl and striped café au lait linen are natural and restful.

Finding the right pictures to hang on the wall, arranging collections of favourite objects, displaying flowers and plants — finishing touches are what bring a room to life. Even in a spare, minimal setting, a few beautiful objects, displayed for their own sake, give a sense of personality and vitality — in fact, the less you put into a room, the more important it is that every piece should be worthy of scrutiny.

In a pure interior, whatever you display should not be too highly coloured or patterned. One or two vivid objects can be very effective, but more than this and the balance will be destroyed. Instead of colour or pattern, concentrate on objects which are interesting because of their form or texture, such as smooth beach stones, unglazed earthenware or rustic baskets. Anything which sparkles and reflects light can also give a pure interior interest and depth. Mirrors, glassware of all kinds, and silver or chrome details add sharp definition and make the most of the available light.

Subtle prints, delicate watercolours and drawings are more at home than splashy oil

Above White spring flowers accentuate the purity of a white room. *Below* A mirror reflects glass, silver and porcelain.

*Above A shimmering table setting of glass, silver, candles, flowers and lace. **Below** A collection of chrome Art Deco teapots.*

paintings or bright graphic posters. You can make a feature of monochrome and restrict the pictures you display to black and white studies. If this is too disciplined, prints with pale tints of colour can be refreshing without distracting the eye and even a few intensely coloured pictures will not be overpowering if they are not on a large scale.

Perhaps the most important details of all are flowers and foliage. Growing plants provide a fresh green accent in an all-white room, maintaining the connection with outdoors; flowers are one of the simplest ways of adding life; dried arrangements are unbeatable sources of textural interest.

There are so many types of white flowers, some of which are also beautifully scented, that keeping to one 'colour' is hardly a restriction. And white flowers come in every shape and size: narcissi, daisies, hyacinths, tulips, roses, arum lilies, snowdrops and lily-of-the-valley are just a few. Cut flowers can be set off with variegated or grey-green foliage — ivy, rue, senecio — or dried branches, seedheads, and dried flowers such as hydrangeas.

Above *A decidedly individual collection of found and adapted objects becomes a*
sculptural display between pairs of French windows, revealing a delight
in contrasting materials — rock crystal, metal, glass, stone and perspex.
By keeping this display minimal, it remains elegant.

Above Details add vitality to a room. Contrasting textures, such as
mirror, frosted glass, silver, porcelain and lace, give a sense of depth. White flowers
are elegant and fresh as well as adding a welcome fragrance — narcissi,
tulips, freesias, snowdrops, lilies and roses.

CONTRASTS

*Modern, urban and up to the minute,
the contrast look is a precision style
which relies on good detailing,
well chosen components and flawless backgrounds.
Sharp oppositions of texture, colour and form
add vitality to rooms
designed to be functional and efficient.*

The French have as much respect for what is new as they have for tradition. Hard-edged and thoroughly modern, this style of sharp contrasts has been adopted enthusiastically by young city-dwellers.

The basis of the style is a marriage between classic designs from the first modern period — by Le Corbusier, Gerrit Rietveld and the Bauhaus, for example — and recent trends in decoration and design such as high-tech and Memphis. Backgrounds stay in the background: plain, neutral colours for walls and ceilings, industrial coverings and new wood or carpet for floors. In this restrained, precise setting, well-chosen objects and furniture are pieces to be admired for their graphic quality, sculptural form and the deliberate opposition of materials such as glass and chrome.

This fundamental contrast of black and white, background and foreground, is supplemented by vivid accents of colour and detail. Splashes of paintbox red, blue or yellow are used to coordinate details such as architraves and pipework; rugs, decorative objects and pictures also display brilliant colour and bold, abstract patterns.

The style depends upon good organization of space, clever arrangements of the components and precision detailing. At one extreme, rooms can be as stark and as minimal as a modern art gallery; at the other, tongue-in-cheek references to Pop culture, 'retro' kitsch from the 1950s and post-modern bric-à-brac suggest a certain playfulness. It is a style which is particularly at home in converted industrial spaces, apartments, open-plan studios and ateliers.

The uncompromising appearance of some of these interiors and the furniture in them can be misleading: Le Corbusier's chaise longue is just as comfortable as a traditional upholstered sofa. The industrial or commercial ancestry of many of the common elements means that they often have an in-built practicality and efficiency; surfaces, for instance, are durable and easy to maintain. Although the best of modern design does not come cheap, two or three classic pieces can be supplemented by good mass-produced and inexpensive furniture without destroying the entire effect. And one special advantage of this style is that the paraphernalia of modern living — kitchen appliances, hi-fi, television and video equipment — are not an unwelcome intrusion. Altogether, the look expresses Le Corbusier's famous saying, that the house should be a 'machine for living in'.

Above left The contrast interior as modern art gallery — the perfect environment for displaying bold, graphic rugs and paintings. *Above right* Strong clashing colours set against a black-and-white background. *Opposite* Precise organization of space is a key feature of the look.

Contrast style is resolutely modern in its references and sources of inspiration,
highly influenced by the work of twentieth-century artists, such as Fernand
Léger, who explored the impact of technology and celebrated or
analyzed the Machine Age. This picture *(above)*, which Léger painted in 1954, is
entitled 'Two Women Holding Flowers'. Surfaces and finishes are
derived from industry and commerce; 'form follows function' is the hallmark of good
design. All types of modern architecture are also powerful references,
from the high-tech tour de force, the Pompidou Centre, with its exposed ducts and
services, to concrete and steel skyscrapers or the elegant geometries of
Art Deco. Nature is an inspiration only at its most severe: desert landscapes, the stiff
'architectural' foliage of palms, the ordered minimal beauty of
Japanese gardens.

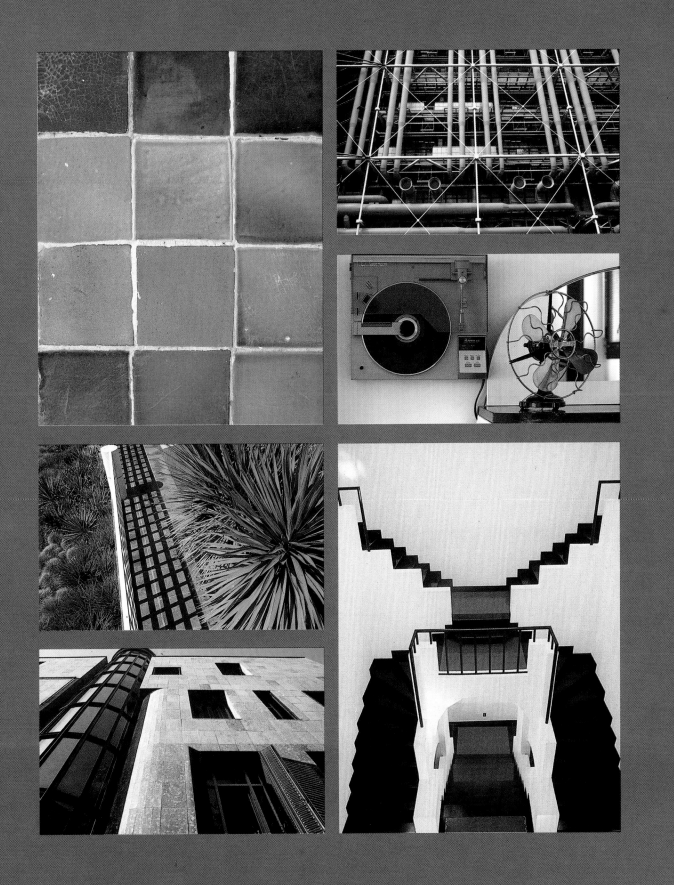

The success of this thoroughly modern look depends, at least in part, on ensuring that the background is flawless. In a modern interior, either signs of wear and tear or the mellowness of age and 'distressed' finishes will lack charm.

For this reason, it is vital to put enough time and effort — if not money — into perfecting the background. Good preparation is essential for a precision finish: walls must be smooth and even, floors should be level, and any cracks and other irregularities will have to be corrected.

Paradoxically, the intention is primarily to make the background inconspicuous and anonymous. Neutral colour schemes and serviceable finishes direct the attention firmly to the furniture and displays which are put into the room, rather than the way the surfaces are decorated.

Top The contrast of wood, tiling and carpeting is further underlined by the asymmetric, stepped design of this bathroom. Above Walls painted a sandy colour tone with the parquet floor lending warmth to an elegant 1930s-style dining room.

THE PALETTE

In the high-contrast interior, colour is used as a decorative feature rather than as a means of generating atmosphere. Blocks of bright colour or individual accents — on details such as door handles, decorative objects, pictures and rugs — are highlighted against neutral backdrops. This graphic way of using colour is reminiscent of the work of the Dutch painter, Piet Mondrian, and the designs of the Constructivists, in which balanced compositions of abstract colour shapes are superimposed on black and white grids. Colours are both vivid and intense. Primary colours, associated with high-tech, are most typical, but in addition to paintbox reds, blues and yellows, there are the post-modern shades of turquoise; hot pink and electric blue. The colours can be so strong because they are confined mainly to small areas and details, and are mediated by larger expanses of white and black, as well as that all-purpose modern colour, grey. Black is a very important element in the modern interior, anchoring the different colour accents and providing a crisp, graphic line which adds definition to neutral backgrounds. In the ultimate contrast room, colour is excluded completely and black is an accent.

One useful strategy is coordination, with a single strong colour selected to unify details, set off against a monochrome background. But a mixture of colour accents also works well, if there is enough breathing space for each colour to be displayed on its own without uncomfortable, jarring clashes. Strong colour accents are particularly suitable for nurseries and children's rooms.

Top left Rainbow radiators, painted in a spectrum — from yellow through orange to red — make a vivid colour detail. *Top right* Soothing aquamarine is given strength and 'punch' by black-and-white linen. *Above* This bright kitchen displays a Mondrian-style use of colour.

Above *Columns of fabric, framing black Venetian blinds, make a striking textural contrast. A checkered rug draws together a seating area.* ***Opposite top*** *Classical motifs used on original black-and-white print fabrics.* ***Opposite below*** *A unity of hard surfaces — tiles, glass and metal.*

PATTERN AND TEXTURE

Like colour, pattern is also 'displayed' in the high-contrast interior, although its use is strictly limited. This has the effect of maximizing the impact. Taking inspiration from modern art and contemporary design, patterns on display are typically abstract, graphic and often asymmetric.

Unlike the traditional way of using pattern as a way of synthesizing colours and themes to blend in with the overall decorative effect, pattern in the modern interior may feature only on one rug or a pair of curtains. For this reason, the pattern should be bold and large in scale so that it functions as a true focus of attention. Forthright designs in black and white, geometric prints, 1950s stylized motifs, repeat images from Pop culture, lettering and other themes derived from graphic design all suit the high-contrast style. However, the only traditional patterns which are compatible with this type of interior are non-figurative ethnic ones, such as the designs of Persian carpets, kilims and dhurries.

With both colour and pattern treated as decorative features, texture becomes an important way of giving modern rooms unity. Contrast interiors are intrinsically 'hard' which can lead people to assume that they are not comfortable. It is true that they lack the impression of softness of more upholstered interiors, for this is a style which relies on the use of inflexible industrial products and materials not commonly used in domestic settings. Tubular steel and moulded plastic are typical rather than

flowing fabric and deep upholstery. But although the textures of these finishes and surfaces do not create an enveloping sense of comfort, they do generate a certain rhythm and vitality which keeps the overall effect from looking too uniform. The sharp oppositions of leather and chrome, glass and studded rubber, laminate and aluminium, are lively while maintaining the crisp, graphic edge essential to the look.

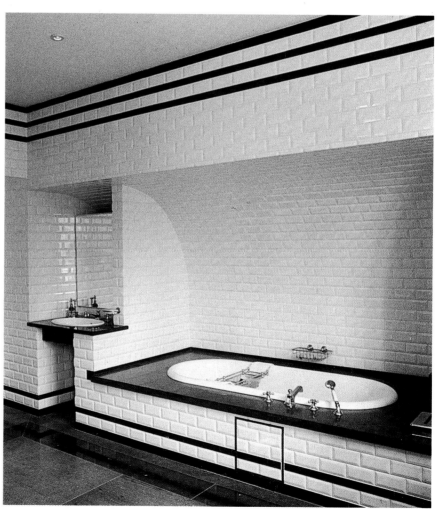

The way in which walls and ceilings are decorated may seem to be the least interesting part of this style, but the quality of these surfaces is nevertheless very important. The classic approach is to treat them like the background in an art gallery — matt white paint used over perfect plaster is often the best solution. It is always worth taking the trouble to ensure that the surface is in good condition before you begin decorating. Once all the imperfections have been corrected, apply the paint in many even coats for the best results.

Aside from white, different shades of grey — from warm pinkish grey to cool grey-blue — make excellent contemporary backdrops. It is not always possible to find the exact colour of grey you want in commercial paint ranges; if this is the case, a grey base coat can be modified by the subtle techniques of sponging or ragging.

Although true modernists rarely put colour on the walls, slightly tinted shades such as blue-green or pink are often features of contemporary post-modern decor. Wall colour can be used to define separate areas within an open-plan space — to accent an alcove, for example, or to distinguish a kitchen corner from the main living area.

Top left A vivid blue-green defines a work area. The window frames are picked out in grey to match the flooring. *Top right* Horizontal battens around the perimeter of the room support a collection of photographs. *Above* Contrast banding highlights architectural detail.

Tiling is always a good solution for kitchen and bathroom walls: the utility look of plain glazed or matt ceramic tiles is particularly appropriate. A variety of effects can be achieved by using different sizes as well as colours of tiles, laying tiles in diagonal patterns, finishing areas with contrasting borders and extending tiling over work surfaces and built-in units. The graphic, gridded appearance of tiling can also be accentuated dramatically by making a feature of the grouting — for example, by adding colour so that the grout shows up against plain white tiling.

For new partition walls, one very striking (although expensive) solution is to use glass bricks. Sculptural and light-filtering, glass bricks make effective room dividers in open-plan areas as well as beautiful, yet practical, bathroom partitions.

Above left The busy grid of small tiles makes a practical finish for a below-stairs storage area. ***Above right*** It takes good planning and careful execution to tile an entire room. Here, the grid on walls, shelves and floor matches perfectly and the result is crisply functional.

In the contrast interior, the floor counts as part of the background and is therefore essentially neutral, unifying and seamless. Products originally designed for office or factory use are often adopted: as well as projecting a machine image, these coverings are also extremely practical and hard-wearing.

The softest option is carpeting, an especially good choice if different areas need to be unified, or if there is a need for sound insulation. The neatly ribbed appearance of cord carpet makes a matt, unobtrusive surface, especially in neutral shades of biscuit or grey. Industrial-weight cord can be a good solution for heavy-traffic areas.

Wood is also a fairly forgiving surface, easy on the eye, warm and traditional. Providing they are in good condition, classic wood floors — parquet, wood strip, tile, and polished as well as black floorboards — are perfectly acceptable in modern rooms and can add a welcome hint of warmth. The rustic charm of old stripped pine, however, is definitely not part of the look. If an existing floor cannot be renovated to a high enough standard, one solution is to paint over the defects.

Sheet flooring — vinyl, linoleum or rubber — looks precise, crisp and suitably utilitarian. Vinyl is a good, practical covering for kitchen and bathroom floors and many plain geometric patterns exist for choice. Linoleum is available in a wide range of colours, including types with metallic or marblized finishes as well as quartz-flecked varieties.

Originally designed for heavy-duty use (particularly for the floors of airports and railway stations), studded rubber has become synonymous with high-tech. Usually relief-patterned, it is extremely hard-wearing but can be difficult to keep clean because dirt tends to build up around the raised textures. Vinyl, linoleum and rubber are also widely used in tile form. Tiles are easier to manage if you want to create patterns with alternating colours or borders.

Harder materials such as ceramic tiles and terrazzo are cool and elegant, and provide a strong sense of geometry. Different effects can be achieved using different sizes of tiles: smaller tiles are busier and suit small areas, larger tiles have a more classic appearance.

Above Tiling provides the opportunity to create pattern, such as this classic black-and-white checkered floor. **Opposite** The Mediterranean coolness and simplicity of a white ceramic-tiled floor ensures that nothing distracts the eye from the lush garden view.

RUGS

In recent years, there has been a resurgence of interest in modern textile design with the result that there is a wide range of contemporary rugs currently being produced. In addition to the work of new designers, there are good reproductions of classic modern designs available, such as those created by Eileen Gray in the late 1920s for her house at Roquebrune in France.

Contemporary rugs make excellent centre-pieces for modern living rooms. They take the edge off all the hard surfaces and also provide important visual anchors for the layout of furniture, defining conversation areas and adding a floor-level focus of interest.

Top A blue-and-white checkered rug adds bold colour to an otherwise monochromatic room, thereby defining the fireplace as a focal point. **Above** Rugs by contemporary designers can amount to art at floor level, as this abstract, painterly design demonstrates.

Top left Blocks of soft colour on a modern rug add interest to a neutral colour scheme. *Top right* The strikingly asymmetric design of this rug is echoed in the furniture layout. *Above* Constructivist graphics provide the inspiration for a dining-area rug.

Just as an immaculate finish is important for surfaces such as walls, floors and ceilings, windows which are of good quality can be a considerable asset in a high-tech interior. The perfect square or rectangle may be an ideal, but existing windows can often be improved just by paying attention to detail such as the direction of architraves and glazing bars. In the modern interior, it is more difficult to hide an ugly window behind layers of drapery: cosmetic cover-ups are at odds with the entire style. Uncovered windows, especially those which are unusual or striking in appearance, suit the graphic look.

Utilitarian, sleek and versatile, the Venetian blind has become a classic element in the modern interior. Originally devised for office and commercial use, designs have now been modified and the colour range extended to offer a wider choice of styles and materials for the home. Venetian blinds are available in metal (aluminium), plastic and wood; in pastels, primaries and metallic shades; with pierced, wide or narrow slats; and with coordinating cords and rails. They can be manufactured to fit almost any size of opening, making a particularly good solution for large picture windows, and they can even be used as room

dividers. The slats can be adjusted to vary the degree of light admitted — an advantage since the effect of light slanting through half-open blinds is evocative and atmospheric.

But softer treatments, relying on the use of fabric, are not entirely ruled out for this style. Fabric can be a good way of introducing blocks of solid colour or of displaying geometric or abstract patterns. Roller blinds or Roman blinds, which pleat up into neat, horizontal folds, are crisp-looking and understated. Simple curtains in plain fabrics and with tailored headings will blend in well with a neutral background; a length of boldly patterned fabric, pulled back to one side in an asymmetric arrangement, will inject a touch of drama without looking too cluttered.

And it can be worth experimenting with more unusual solutions. In a bathroom, for example, replacing clear window glass with frosted glass maintains privacy and keeps the look simple. Screens — panels covered in semi-transparent cloth — can either be fixed in place to the frame or else left standing in front of a window. Vertical fabric louvres, which pivot to allow the filtering of light, are another useful import from commercial design.

Above A folding screen in glass filters light. **Right** A huge plate-glass picture window screened with fine Venetian blinds.

Above left Venetian blinds provide privacy in a spectacular sky-lit bedroom. *Above* Ingenious fabric blinds on runners cut down overhead glare.

In keeping with the contrast style, lighting is used in a sharply defined way, and is dramatic and undiffused. The crisp, white light of halogen is a definite advantage in a modern interior but low-voltage fluorescent can also be successful.

In the contrast interior, a light fitting has all the status of a design object. While it may be technically sophisticated, spare and uncluttered, it is ultimately sculptural, an object to be admired.

The notion that form should follow function — an important tenet of modern design philosophy — is particularly evident in light-fitting design. Lighting

systems and individual designs have been borrowed from offices, factories and photographic studios where fittings are usually defined by the job they do rather than by their appearance. Black, white and chrome are universal colours; metal, plastic and glass are typical materials.

In any interior it is important to have a mixture of general or background illumination and more directional 'task' lighting. Uplighters, either floor-standing or wall-mounted, are effective sources of background light in a contrast interior. Although directional, as the term 'uplighter' suggests, they

Top left A black task light accents a mantlepiece display. *Top right* Opaque
bulbs surrounding a bathroom mirror provide glare-free lighting.
Above left Sculptural column uplights. *Above right* A modern classic —
the 'Jill' floor-standing uplighter.

bounce light off the ceiling and thus raise the general level of illumination in the room. Large photographic reflectors directed upwards do the same job. In addition, there are many modern pendant fittings, ubiquitous downlighters and spotlights available. Spotlights have become such a feature of modern interiors that it is hard to remember that they were originally commercial products.

In the area of task or accent lighting there has been a great refinement of desk lamps, such as the classic Anglepoise, over recent years. There are many options, both decorative and practical, to replace the more traditional table lamps including adjustable counterweighted designs, arced lights and mini halogen spotlights with dichroic reflectors.

In recent years, Italy and other European countries have been at the forefront of lighting design. Firms such as Artemide, Arteluce, Flos and Tronconi have been responsible for many modern classics including the 'Jill' floor-standing uplighter and the Tizio task light. At this level, fittings are not cheap, but there is now a whole range of alternative light fittings which produce the same effect available from some of the leading chain-stores.

Top left Versatile counterweighted task lights for reading or background lighting.
Top right Track lighting has a forthright, functional look. **Above left**
A wall-mounted uplight gives discreet background lighting. **Above right** A modern
pendant fitting makes an elegant overhead light.

Both formal and disciplined, the contrast style relies on the ability to understand the way space is used. Therefore, the layout of rooms and furniture is more important and needs to be more precise than it is in other more cluttered and casual styles. And, paradoxically, although the emphasis is on function, individual pieces of furniture tend to stand in rooms as if they were like modern sculpture in an art gallery.

Contrast style represents a search for perfection, perfection both of space and of all it contains. Early modern designers expected such perfection to be achieved via mass production, but this expectation was largely unfulfilled. It was not until the late 1970s, when the high-tech style became popular, that an interest in machine-made goods was reawakened. This, in turn, has led to a renewed appreciation of design ideas from the early modern period between the wars.

Top Furniture layout can be one way of distinguishing different activities within a multi-purpose area. Here, the sense of space is emphasized by open doorways. *Above* Art Deco-style leather armchairs, supplemented by a pair of folding cinema seats.

THE LAYOUT

A modern style of furnishing works well in urban settings — apartments, converted industrial spaces such as lofts or ateliers or places where there is the opportunity to move away from conventional room arrangements are all ideal. In particular, an ambiguous or open-plan area which does not dictate a set layout will benefit from this approach.

Rather than relying simply on assigning different activities to different rooms — dining, sleeping, living and so on — it is important with this style to first consider the qualities of a particular area, together with your needs, and then to arrange the furniture and facilities to suit. Before you begin, it is a good idea to consider how the traffic will flow; for example, the routes between dining and kitchen areas or bedrooms and bathrooms. You should also plan storage very carefully and take into account special interests which need work or hobby areas.

Furniture layout in the contrast interior is usually based on some type of implicit geometric grid.

Symmetry is important and there should be enough room for each piece to stand out clearly. In practice, this often means having rather less furniture than in traditional rooms. The difficulty with this type of sparse, precise arrangement, however, is that areas of rooms can fail to cohere, and the furniture can appear to 'float' uncomfortably in space. The remedy for this problem is to create focal points to anchor the layout — a fireplace, a vivid rug or even a floor-level arrangement of objects can all be useful ways to define areas.

There are several ways to create distinct areas in a large open space without sacrificing the original proportions and scale. These include dividing the room with free-standing shelf units, or adding partitions such as half-height counters, glass brick walls, Venetian blinds or folding screens. Alternatively, you can build a shallow platform at one end of the room to serve as a dining area or kitchen. A more permanent solution, especially good in a room with high ceilings, is to build a gallery at one end to act as a bedroom or study.

Above The overriding atmosphere is modern despite the inclusion of older pieces of furniture. The classical simplicity of the Empire-style bench blends well with a modern uplighter. Sofas are transformed by swathes of red drapery, an effective contrast to the crisp floor.

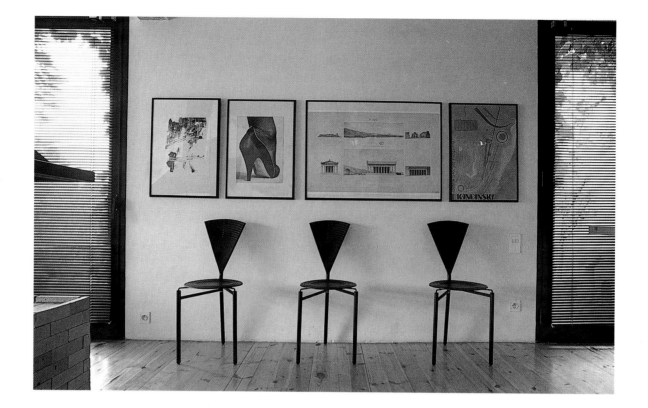

Top *These modern chairs are designed to be looked at as much as to be sat upon.* **Above** *An updated version of a day bed for comfortable seating.*

There is a considerable amount of choice when it comes to furnishing the contrast interior. At one end of the scale, there are classic designs from the early part of the century, by designers such as Le Corbusier, Mies van der Rohe, and Rietveld; at the other, there are many affordable, practical and good looking mass-produced pieces, no less 'designed', but lacking the status of cult objects. The pure lines of early modernism can be supplemented either by using the witty and colourful Memphis-style furniture or with the severity of high-tech designs.

Although the best examples of modern furniture design are every bit as expensive as fine antiques, a few good pieces are enough to achieve the effect as the look is essentially 'underfurnished'. The Le Corbusier chaise longue and 'Grand Confort' armchair (1928), Rietveld's 'Red-Blue' chair (1917), Mies van der Rohe's cantilever chair (1927) and 'Barcelona' chair (1929), and Marcel Breuer's 'Model B33' chair (1930) have become synonymous with the modern interior. These pieces, with their clean lines and innovative form, look as startling and original today as when they were first conceived. Other more recent examples, which can be admired as much as used, include a range of contemporary designs from the Italian firm Cassina, such as the

'Wink' chair, which resembles a piece of soft sculpture, or Scandinavian modern classics, such as Arne Jacobsen's 'Egg' chair featuring a curved upholstered seat like an empty shell.

These designs are all worthy of attention and demand enough space to be appreciated properly: too many 'designer objects' in a room can be overpowering. To supplement such pieces it is a good idea to opt for other understated and serviceable furniture, such as simple metal or wooden folding or stacking chairs — the type of designs used in restaurants or cafés — all flexible and comfortable products which can serve as additional living-room seating, dining-chairs or work chairs. Plain, upholstered benches and futons are other affordable seating alternatives.

Tables are simple, inspired by commercial designs or sometimes improvised. For instance, a sheet of reinforced or wired glass on a metal framework is crisp without looking dominant; black lacquered wood or laminate also gives a strong graphic line; a formica top on coloured trestles or a Kee Klamp frame adds a touch of high-tech. Angular tables with bright paint-spattered finishes are a Memphis inspiration and can add vivid colour accents to a contrast room.

Above Gerrit Rietveld's 'Red-Blue' chair dates from 1917. *Left* Black leather and chrome furniture are modern classics.

STORAGE

Storage is one aspect of the contrast interior where the influence of the industrial and commercial world is particularly apparent. Although strict modernists prefer everyday clutter stored well out of sight, building in enough cupboard space behind the scenes can sometimes be expensive and impractical. The alternatives, which owe a great deal to the high-tech approach, consist of a range of efficient, adaptable systems borrowed from offices, factories and shops. Most are relatively cheap, are suitable for different applications and can be taken apart when you move.

For shelving, there is always the office stand-by — a system of notched aluminium tracks which support metal brackets. Shelves can be either reinforced glass, painted wood, or MDF (medium-density fibreboard) which is stable across wide spans. Free-standing wire shelving is another

commercial product, but it can be more expensive. Alternatives to traditional wardrobes or chests of drawers include clothes rails or metal lockers for hanging space, wire baskets for folding clothes and shoes, and wire-mesh grids for accessories. Alcoves fitted with shelves, rails and sliding baskets can be screened from view with blinds which also help to keep clothes free from dust and fading.

Wire-mesh trolleys are useful for accommodating electronic equipment, television, video and hi-fi systems or else they can serve as movable home offices carrying computer terminals or typewriters. Filing cabinets are also versatile: aside from housing household or home-office paperwork, there are narrow drawered versions which can be used in kitchens, bedrooms or workrooms for utensils, accessories and tools. In the kitchen, fitted units can be supplemented with wire stacking baskets for storing vegetables or cookware; metal racks or butchers' rails can be added for suspending utensils.

Top left Open kitchen shelves, racks and rails make beautiful and efficient storage.
Above left The clothes rail, originally a shop fitting, is a practical solution to the shortage of hanging space. *Above right* Office cabinets given a lacquered finish. *Opposite* Modular shelving provides a wall of storage.

Contrast style is an approach for the whole interior, so it is difficult to combine this look with other types of decoration and furnishing. But it is possible to change the emphasis from room to room. Bright colours can be played up in a child's room, whereas form and shape can take priority in a living room.

Kitchens are areas which are naturally sympathetic to modern design. Fitted units, appliances and built-in worktops create a functional, working environment which can be accentuated by plain surfaces and decoration. Equally modern is the use of bright primary colours for a cheerful, irreverent look. One particular benefit is that appliances and kitchen equipment do not need to be disguised or hidden: being part of the machine image, they fit perfectly into the contrast style.

In the same way, bathrooms can be overtly functional, either sleek, seamless and streamlined or accented with dramatic colour. Comfort arises out of efficiency and clean lines rather than traditional bathroom furnishings.

Contrast style may seem at odds in the bedroom, conventionally decorated in a soft, upholstered way. However, lack of ornament and pure, uncluttered form is just as effective at providing a sense of peace and tranquillity as a more traditional approach. Alternatively, bright bedcovers, high-tech details and hard-edged furnishing can be a good way of decorating a sleeping area which also has to serve as a study. Because it is intrinsically formal, the contrast style also suits dining rooms or dining areas; in living areas, one particular advantage of the style is that there is no need to banish the television, video or stereo system.

Top A dramatic double-height living area, furnished in black. **Above left** Studded rubber flooring and industrial storage bins — the influence of high-tech. **Above right** Eclectic modernism. **Opposite above** Classic urban style. **Opposite below** Delight in geometric form.

Right *A playful post-modern living room, with Memphis coffee table and cabinet. White leather upholstery and ivory walls provide a neutral background to set off the more idiosyncratic pieces. Plasterwork mouldings picked out in gold and pale blue make a witty detail.*
Below *A serene modern room with a great sense of calm. Lack of planning, poor finishes or awkward details would be glaring in such a minimal space.*

Left The half-height divider in this open-plan living and dining room is emphasized by the columns picked out in mint green. Black metal and white cotton are crisp and contrasting in this airy, comfortable space.
Below A hard-edged modern conversion makes dramatic use of scale and proportion, an ideal environment for the display of modern art. This beautifully detailed gallery stair has its own sculptural quality, delineating the far wall.

Above *A grey-spattered paint finish, matching the granite worktop, makes a comfortable transition between the pale floor, white ceiling and matt-black fitted units. Advances in the design of units and appliances make the kitchen a quintessentially modern room.*

Above This dining alcove, which accompanies the kitchen on the facing page, is
strikingly lit by a wall-mounted tube, and enjoys a view of the stairway
via an oversized circular window. The hard materials of metal and glass are softened
by a superb wooden floor and rug.

Left A well-planned bathroom, with pristine tiled surfaces. The utility look is emphasized by exposed metal joists and the commercial light fitting over the double basins. *Below* A careful composition in black, white, red and grey demonstrates the effectiveness of extending contrast style to a bedroom. *Bottom* Bold striped bed linen maintains a sense of modernity and order in this studio bedroom. The floor-level mattress and light make an easy conversion from day- to night-time use. *Opposite* A vibrant colour theme throughout the room makes a virtue out of simplicity. Lack of clutter and pure lines promote an Eastern-style tranquillity which is particularly appropriate in a bedroom.

Although this is not a cluttered look, details such as decorative objects, pictures and plants can make or mar the effect. Details are not only important as a means of adding colour and pattern to what might otherwise be too stark and severe, they also help to alleviate the strict discipline and control of the style by injecting a sense of life and the unexpected.

Architectural detail — architraves, skirting boards, doors and dado rails — can be a useful way of unifying a series of modern rooms. Frames or handles picked out in a single colour emphasize the graphic approach, especially when the rest of the background is resolutely neutral.

Decorative objects can be bold, bright and bizarre. Modern ceramics, old metal toys, kitsch junk from the 1950s, packaging and odd found objects all have a certain surprise element. At the other

Top A collection of model airplanes in a corner below the stairs makes a witty welcome in a hallway. **Above** *Cacti, strelitzia, pure white tulips, long-stemmed freesias and a bowl of lemons are the perfect accompaniment to this modern living room.*

extreme are pure modern pieces, such as classic Scandinavian glass bowls and vases (particularly those by Alvar Aalto), the ubiquitous matt black designer objects or plain white porcelain bowls.

The graphic element can be played up by hanging a collection of black-and-white prints or photographs on the wall. Large framed posters, modern paintings and brilliant hangings all add colour and drama.

The best plants to choose are those which are large enough to stand singly and which have defined, rather 'architectural' foliage. Ficus, yucca and many varieties of palm suit modern interiors better than groups of softer-looking flowering plants. Similarly, flower arrangements should be bold and coordinated; spiky winter branches, seedheads and leaves also look dramatic.

Top Strelitzia in a tangerine vase set on an ingenious high-tech display shelf, harmonizes with the colours displayed in the painting. ***Above*** Red roses cut short in an Alvar Aalto vase provide the sole colour accent in a monochrome room with its modern marble fireplace.

Above *A period window with its stained glass medallions has an appropriately Gothic flavour which suits the collection of off-beat, surreal objects and furniture. The miniature umbrella looks like a lampshade, completing the idiosyncratic arrangement.*

Above *Accessories, decorative objects, flowers and other details can be an important means of adding colour to a contrast room. Brightly coloured glassware or crockery, coordinated door and cupboard handles, can all supply the necessary vivid accents.*

HARMONY

The harmony style is for those
who revel in colour and pattern,
are intrigued by the unusual and idiosyncratic
and have an affection for the past.
Town or country,
the look is traditional and relaxed,
but the flair for arrangement
and the instinctive sense of co-ordination
is unmistakably French.

The French have always been admired for a certain genius, best described as *art de vivre*, or style as a way of life. It is the unconscious ability to synthesize influences from different sources and periods, traditional and regional, old and new, into a harmonious whole. In practice, it involves an instinct for arrangement, a Bohemian flair for making something out of nothing and the confidence to mix colours and patterns sympathetically.

With this approach, there can be a strong undercurrent of nostalgia in the way that rooms are put together and decorated, but this is nostalgia for a vague, ill-defined past, not a slavish devotion to restoration or reproduction. Signs of wear are tolerated, even cherished, and family heirlooms can coexist happily with flea-market bargains.

The look is, above all, eclectic. There are traditional elements, and these express the diversity and vitality of French regional styles. The Far East, India and Africa are more exotic reference points; the countryside and rural life are abiding sources of inspiration. This *mélange* of influences, however, stops short of resulting in the kind of hodge-podge of an old curiosity shop: editing is all important.

The basic decorating strategy is one of coordination. Because the aim is to achieve the warmth and conviviality of a family home, this is not a lifeless, relentless matching of colour and pattern, but instead an approach which relies on an affinity of tone and design. This look is not imposed on its surroundings and has the appearance of being not really 'finished', accommodating easily the occasional surprise or happy accident.

It can, however, be urban and sophisticated, despite its rural associations and, in this respect, it differs from its English counterpart, the country house style. This is partly to do with the fact that there are certain time-honoured classic elements — copper-bottomed pots and pans, traditional handprinted fabrics, decorative tiles, open shelves of china, wrought ironwork and lace panels — which work equally well in either the town or the country.

Essentially comfortable and welcoming, this style is particularly suited to family life, for those on a small budget or for people who expect to furnish and decorate a home piece by piece over the years. There is always room for expressions of individual taste such as personal treasures, collections of curios, the unusual and the idiosyncratic. A flexible approach rather than a style, the harmonious interior is a celebration of the beauty of familiar and everyday things.

Above left Antique lace and the fine period mirror are richly decorative.
Above right Cool eau-de-nil *walls provide the background for a mantelpiece display of dried flowers and bric-à-brac.* **Opposite** *Distressed apricot walls and marbled mouldings in a family dining room.*

*France has a wealth of regional styles, expressed in its vernacular architecture and
the traditional designs of fabric, ceramics and basketwork, all of which
can provide a rich source of ideas and inspiration for colour, pattern and textural
combinations. Relying on handmade rather than mass-produced objects,
natural rather than synthetic materials and the informal rather than the grand,
harmony style is a celebration of the simple life at its best.*

True harmony interiors tend to evolve over the years as surfaces mellow and patterns are added layer by layer until there is a comfortable blend of different finishes, colours and textures. But this approach is, in fact, far from haphazard: it demands the ability to keep a particular vision in mind, to select and edit from a wide range of options, and to resist the temptation to impose a finished look on a room regardless of its character.

Whether you intend to decorate a room from scratch or to just put it together gradually, it is important to work out an overall scheme to direct your choice. You can go to the extent of making up a scheme board of fabric swatches, paint colours, and samples of wallpaper or flooring in order to see how all the elements will work in practice. This may sound rather deliberate — a 'decorated' rather than a decorative approach — but it can be treated as a strategy rather than a blueprint.

THE PALETTE

Colours in the harmony interior are rich, strong and enveloping, a means of generating atmosphere and mood. Inspiration can be found in the drifting colours of country gardens and landscapes, in the work of Impressionist painters such as Monet and Seurat, and in the glowing colour combinations found in traditional prints on fabrics, ceramics and wallpaper.

Colours are often categorized as either 'warm' or 'cool'. Warm shades include burgundy, terracotta, burnt orange and peach; cool colours range from *eau de nil*, dove grey, azure and mint green to the classic French blue. This type of classification can be a useful rule-of-thumb when choosing a colour scheme for a particular room. Because colour can be used on a large scale, it is important to pick shades which will enhance a room's natural qualities such as its proportion and the amount of light it receives. Cool colours reflect light and are a useful way of increasing the impression of size, and this suits rooms which receive a good deal of natural light, especially south-facing ones. Warm colours cheer up darker areas and generate a sense of enclosure and intimacy.

It is important to use colour in a way that has subtlety and depth; this means opting for soft mid-shades rather than strident primaries or bold contrasts. Depth can also be achieved by colour coordination. On a small scale, it can be charming to repeat one colour on several elements, for instance, on the walls, upholstery and details, but

Above A mosaic floor, elaborately carved architraves, a panelled dado and the rich stained-glass door provide a wealth of detail and interest in a hallway. A distressed paint finish — a stylized version of marbling — adds to the sense of depth in a narrow space.

this strict matching needs to be handled with skill or the result will look lifeless and claustrophobic. It is often better to assemble several closely related shades which have varying tones so that there is inherent modulation and variety in the scheme. For additional definition and variety, details such as curtain trimmings or piping can be in a sharply contrasting accent colour which serves to add vitality and throw the coordinated scheme into relief. This treatment tends to work most effectively if only one or two colours are chosen: the aim is for a rigorous, sharp look which brings life to an interior, and not a series of fighting tones.

Using neutral shades can be a successful way of mediating between areas of pattern or strong colour. Chalky whites, cream and the natural shades of stone, biscuit or ecru are all intrinsically warmer than modern monochromes.

Top left Eau de nil *unifies all the wooden surfaces — cupboard, panelling and fire surround — offset by fresh white walls.* **Above left** Colour-washed walls in green and terracotta for an aged, mellow look. **Above right** A mural of a tropical garden promotes an exotic atmosphere.

PATTERN AND TEXTURE

Above all, this style is decorative and much of the enjoyment and enthusiasm of the look is expressed in the use of pattern. In terms of fabric, there is a rich source of both traditional prints and ethnic designs to choose from, ranging through classic French patterns such as *toile de Jouy,* Provençal *Souleiado,* or the tone on tone designs of Jacquard linens, to lace, paisleys, plaids, simple checks or oriental *ikats.* But pattern can also be expressed in floor design — checkered tile floors, oriental rugs, parquet — or in details such as wrought ironwork, plaster mouldings, displays of china and screens.

The simplest way of using pattern is to treat it as a feature, allowing enough visual breathing space for it to be displayed fully, for example, by having patterned curtains, or a rich rug, or printed upholstery. Greater depth can be achieved by setting off plain areas with patterned details, such as printed borders, painted friezes or decorative tiles framing walls or floors. But the most intricate approach is to build up layers of separate patterns in order to blend different surfaces together and create a sense of rhythm. For different patterns to combine effectively, however, they must display some kind of affinity. For instance, you can match a floral pattern with a fine stripe which picks out one of the colours in the print or you can use the same pattern twice — once with the motif reversed out or smaller in scale. Alternatively, you can layer traditional patterns that share common colours such as paisleys or plaids. It is important, however, to know where to stop: too many large-scale, dramatic or brightly coloured patterns in a room will compete for attention, and the look will become confusing and cluttered.

The use of texture in the harmony interior is a way of expressing a connection with the countryside, rustic life and the past. A sense of forthright simplicity and charm can be evoked with handmade 'peasant' ware, or with natural surfaces such as stone, brick, wood and wicker. Liveliness and depth can be achieved by contrasting hard surfaces (etched glass, mirror, polished copper or wrought iron) with soft ones (lace, muslin, silk shawls or embroidered cloths). In a country setting, the rough textures of unglazed terracotta pots, wicker baskets, bunches of drying herbs and scrubbed tables are especially suitable, being both rural and nostalgic.

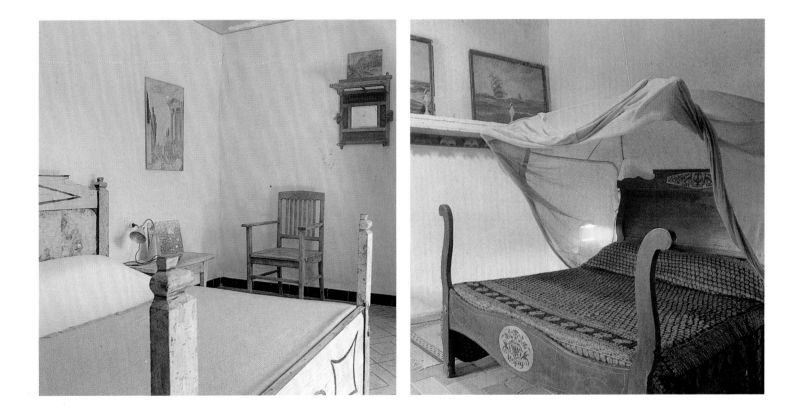

Above left Cool shades of pale turquoise and primrose yellow in a period setting.
Above right Canary yellow walls make a vivid backdrop for an antique
bedstead. Opposite A collection of blue-and-white china is the basis for a fresh and
charming dining-room colour scheme.

The aim of this pleasingly relaxed style is to achieve comfort rather than perfection. Pristine surfaces, in fact, can look glaring and out of place. However, gentle decay is better than outright decrepitude. In terms of decoration, depth equals the desired patina of age, either artificial or real.

There are many ways to achieve subtlety with a painted finish, all of which avoid the unwanted spick and span appearance of new decoration. One way is the careful choice of colour. Softer, pastel or secondary shades provide a natural recession that has more depth than the bright, graphic look of pure, clear colours. There is also a whole range of paint techniques which can be used to 'break up' the surface area of a wall so that the final finish is never flat. Diluting the paint to create a wash, applying it unevenly with a tool such as a sponge or a rag, spattering, or mixing over glazes and tints with artists' colours are all methods of avoiding a freshly painted look. Successive layers of paint, each slightly different in tone or shade, can be built up to create a glowing, translucent surface. Whitewash, distemper or plain raw plaster finished with a protective sealant also make warm, harmonious wall finishes. But it is important to avoid any overtly stylized paint effects: ragrolling or marbling a large area can be too insistent and obvious for a harmonious effect.

Panelling, stone, brickwork or beams can all be left exposed to contribute to the homely look. Traditional architectural details such as dados, picture rails, cornices, mouldings and architraves are prized features and can often be restored if absent. Tiles are more decorative than utilitarian: they make attractive borders in bathrooms and kitchens and around fireplaces.

Wallpaper is a traditional treatment which is very much part of the look: demure floral patterns are a good choice for bedrooms; turn-of-the-century twining leaf or vine patterns suit dining rooms, studies and entrances; narrow stripes, damask or chinoiserie motifs work well in formal living rooms. Rich tapestry patterns can give a room a decorative print-on-print look, of the kind which can be seen in the background of paintings by Matisse, Bonnard and Vuillard. Because papering a room encloses it, this treatment is a good way of accentuating the small scale of bathrooms, especially when angles and corners are crisply defined by borders or friezes.

Above *Paint effects are good ways of providing a sense of depth and rhythm as this densely stippled wall demonstrates.*

Top Rough natural finishes: raw plaster, stonework and wood. *Above* Traditional blue-and-white tiles.
Left A subtle wallpaper design in grey, white and apricot is elegantly bordered with braid.

In the harmony interior, flooring is used not so much as a means of unifying areas but more as a way to distinguish between them. Different surfaces can change the mood from room to room, introduce textural variety and make interesting interior views.

In each area of the home there are certain classic solutions. Black-and-white checkered tiles (marble, synthetic or ceramic) are the hallmark of the traditional French kitchen. Alternatives, for a warm country look, are quarry tiling and natural stone slabs, both of which age beautifully. Mosaic tiling has the same sort of resonance in the bathroom, in black and white, pale green or cream and white. Brickwork, stone, slate and tiling often feature in hallways, making a practical entrance floor that accepts the wear and tear of traffic from outdoors. Terrazzo and marble are more sophisticated versions of hard flooring most suitable for urban, rather than rural, settings.

In main living areas the traditional flooring is either parquet or polished or painted floorboards. Existing wooden floors may need to be renovated by sanding to remove old layers of varnish or paint and then sealing with coats of varnish or wax. There is also a wide range of new wooden flooring available — block, strip, tile and mosaic — in hardwoods and softwoods. The natural warmth of wood, its ability to combine well with any colour scheme and the way it mellows with time make it an indispensable element of this particular style.

Wooden floors also provide a good surface for the display of rugs. Antique rugs of all descriptions, from fine oriental treasures to handmade rag rugs or needlepoint runners, can act as a foundation for a decorative scheme, suggesting colours which can then be picked out in upholstery and paint finishes. On hard surfaces, such as wooden or stone floors, rugs should always be secured by placing them over a rubber underlay. This ensures that they do not slip or form unsightly wrinkles.

Natural fibres such as coir, sisal and seagrass are good choices for stair carpeting or for laying wall-to-wall in living areas. These materials also serve as good bases for rugs, and make hardwearing but attractive solutions for garden rooms and hallways.

Above left Bricks laid in sweeping circular patterns make a beautiful and mellow entrance floor. *Above right* Two types of traditional flooring: parquet, and stone inset with marble. *Opposite* Herringbone parquet creates a subtle pattern in this dining room.

The use of fabric has traditionally been an important part of French decoration. In the past, Paris was the fashionable centre of upholstery skills, where craftsmen created elaborate confections in silks, damasks and velvets. In the harmony style, although the element of grandeur is missing, the same enjoyment of fabric still remains, even if cotton has replaced other more luxurious materials as a less expensive alternative.

Curtains, in all their many forms, are a natural choice for the harmony interior. They provide the opportunity to unify decorative themes by repeating patterns or colours, they generate a sense of warmth and intimacy, and the flowing folds of fabric add movement and liveliness to any interior.

In a country setting, plain styles work best. Simple, gathered headings suspended from wooden poles are an effective solution. In the city, especially if the architectural detail is particularly grand, more formal drapery may be needed. Lengths of fabric sweeping the floor, Empire-style draped pelmets for a theatrical effect, or the neat elegance of pencil pleats are all good solutions.

Above left Arched double doors, with their glazing bars painted black, create the effect of a Japanese screen. **Top right** *Filmy muslin shirred on a fine rod makes a romantic window treatment.* **Above right** *A kitchen casement window is picked out in bright blue.*

Older houses often incorporate a variety of different window styles such as French windows, square casements or arched windows. As with the purity style, if the window is particularly beautiful and there is no overwhelming need for privacy, it can be a good idea to leave it uncovered. The window can be transformed into a decorative feature by painting the woodwork — the architraves, glazing bars, and shutters — a vivid colour. Alternatively, French windows can be covered in panels of translucent fabric such as lace, muslin or fine cotton, shirred at the top and at the bottom on fine metal rods. A similar treatment will work for casement windows.

The crisp lines of Roman or roller blinds are not at odds with the style, although they suit urban interiors rather better than country ones. Roman blinds can either be plain, trimmed with contrast banding to pick up on colours used in the decoration, or they can work well in striped fabrics and dense, intricate prints. And blinds in natural materials such as cane make evocative light screens for rooms which receive a good deal of direct sun as well as creating a continental atmosphere.

Top left Shutters frame a garden view. *Above left* A kitchen window is filled with shelves carrying a homely collection of storage jars, herbs and glassware, stored conveniently away from work-surfaces. *Above right* Natural split-cane blinds filter light and screen views.

Subtle, flattering and atmospheric, lighting in the harmony interior is not expressly functional but more concerned with creating a congenial mood. The ideal is firelight — from candles or from the hearth — and the closest artificial approximation is the warm tone supplied by tungsten.

To achieve a soft, intimate look, it is important to avoid bright, glaring overhead light. Instead, create overlapping pools of light which lead the eye from area to area. Low pendants over dining tables and well-shaped table lamps beside chairs and sofas boost the light level where it is needed without resulting in a dull, uniform look. For discreet background lighting, choose opaque glass globes or wall lights, such as traditional sconces, and fit dimmer switches so that the light levels can be finely adjusted to suit the occasion.

The style of the light fitting, whether plain or more decorative, is faintly retro in flavour. Art Nouveau and Art Deco lights with sinuous curved metal and glass shades are popular; bistro globes, plain metal pendants and curved brass library lamps are all simple without looking hard-edged. However, it is not necessary to hunt out original fittings: many modern reproductions of these designs are now available at a reasonable price.

Table lamps are indispensable. Decorative ceramic bases can add another pattern detail and fabric shades in pale cream or pink can suffuse a room in a warming glow.

The fireplace provides a natural focal point in this style. Firelight and candlelight can be used to supplement artificial light sources and inject a sense of romance and theatre.

Above Four plain table lamps, arranged at the four corners of a living room, define conversation areas and supply atmospheric, flattering light. The mirror over the fireplace reflects a window, maximizing the effect of natural light inside the room.

Top A dining table lit by a traditional glass pendant — one very acceptable form of overhead lighting. **Above left** *The light from a floor level Art Nouveau lamp is supplemented by firelight.* **Above right** *Wall lights, such as this sinuous metal and glass Art Nouveau design, are widely available.*

In the harmony interior, the emphasis is on comfort, warmth and conviviality — the ideal qualities of a family home. But, despite the apparent lack of formality and the disregard for absolute perfection in decoration, there is nevertheless a certain art to furnishing and arrangement. Without an eye for detail and a flair for combining pieces from different sources, the result could end up looking like a meaningless jumble. Although this look expresses nostalgia for the past, it is never shabby.

Because the ultimate aim is to achieve a natural feeling — as if the rooms had always been furnished in such a way — a rigid adherence to a particular period of decoration is not advisable. By combining old with new, junk with treasures and curios with beautiful objects, you can arrive at a style which expresses a strong sense of personality and which will continue to evolve over the years.

Room layout is never strict or formal: furniture is organized around activities rather than displayed like distinct objects in space. Even in the simpler versions of the style, there is some attempt to make furniture blend in with its surroundings by using throws, print upholstery and natural finishes. The central issue is how best a room can be used and the final arrangement may materialize only after trial and error.

*Above Painted wicker garden chairs have a nostalgic appeal. **Opposite** A comfortable family room, with piles of books and mementoes.*

As far as choosing furniture is concerned, the most important skill required is the ability to blend pieces of different origins, periods and styles.

In general, the simpler the piece the easier it is to integrate. Very ornate nineteenth-century furniture, for example, does not combine well with furniture from other periods. To achieve a feeling of the past it is not necessary to collect fine, grand antiques. Simple rustic pieces and revamped flea-market bargains are equally effective at conveying the mood and are much cheaper.

Plain country furniture — rush-seated chairs, scrubbed refectory tables, blanket chests, pine chests of drawers and open-shelved dressers — all have a forthright, honest appearance as well as being eminently practical. Good modern versions of these simple pieces are available commercially, but originals are still affordable and easy to find. Many have been renovated with stripped and polished finishes, but they can be repainted and even embellished with stencilling if you prefer a more decorated look.

Other time-honoured classics include bent-wood chairs, slatted park chairs, marble-topped bistro tables and Lloyd Loom wickerwork. Beds

Above left The flowing curves of this period sofa are emphasized by the plain powder-blue upholstery. *Above right* Lloyd Loom basket chairs, all in different colours, look informal and cheerful grouped around a marble-topped café table and bring indoors a sense of the garden.

which have bedsteads — wooden, wrought iron or brass — also have a period feel. Basic contemporary pieces, such as comfortable upholstered sofas and armchairs in simple clearcut designs, are now widely available and are easy on the eye and undemanding. Cane furniture, floor cushions and Eastern-style divans for lounging suggest more exotic influences.

Apart from some basic DIY skills which you will need in order to renovate the shabbier items, most of the time and trouble involved in putting this style together will be concerned with finding the pieces in the first place. Auctions, flea markets and junk shops are all typical sources: in general, it is a good idea to avoid more established antique dealers since prices will inevitably be higher. The secret of good bargain hunting is patience and some knowledge of what you are looking for. With experience, it will be easy to distinguish between outright junk and promising pieces which need only minor cosmetic repairs.

Above all, this style is accommodating. Many people set up home with donations from family and friends. The harmonious approach is one of the best ways of reconciling the inevitable collection of different styles *and* making the most of them.

Top A collection of pictures and an inlaid console table lend a touch of refinement to a rustic setting, with its coir matting, rough plastered walls and draped sofa.
Above The simple beauty of wooden country furniture needs little embellishment and matches wooden flooring.

Drapery and soft furnishings not only give a room a rich, upholstered look, but also provide an instant and economical facelift for worn sofas and chairs. Fabric can also soften lines and blend different shapes together. Many of these advantages can be achieved without complicated sewing or upholstery skills, and often the simplest solutions prove to be the most effective.

Second-hand sources are good places to find interesting fabrics at a fraction of the price charged at normal retail outlets. Embroidered cloths, antique shawls and second-hand curtains in fine materials, such as velvet and brocade, can be adapted for a variety of uses and may need only cleaning and minor repairs. Other cheap fabrics include plain cotton sheeting, which can be dyed to match the decoration, and printed Indian bedspreads, which come in rich, intricate patterns.

The easiest way to disguise shabby or faded upholstery, or to cover up a piece of furniture which does not quite fit into the scheme, is to drape it with a length of fabric. Even if there is no need for disguise, paisley shawls, woven throws or blankets give sofas and armchairs a cosy, inviting look. Repeating the sofa fabric on chair-seat cushions (if the sofa and chairs do not match) is a good way of giving visual unity to a scheme.

The bedroom is traditionally an upholstered room and there are many ways of using textiles and fabrics to generate an atmosphere of warmth and softness. In the absence of an interesting bedstead or headboard, kilims or dhurries can be hung on the wall like tapestries; plain fabric shirred on a fine rod behind the bed can also add a touch of drama. Muslin canopies or hangings, such as curtains improvised from cotton bedspreads, can turn the bed into a room within a room. Quilted bedcovers and embroidered bedlinen have great charm.

*Above A Paisley shawl draped over a
sleigh bed.* **Left** *Fabric can
coordinate colours: here, an ochre quilt
tones with yellow walls.*

Harmony style is very much based on the typical and traditional layouts of houses. Rooms are defined by specific activities and have their own distinct atmospheres rather than being open-plan and multi-purpose. For this reason, you can decorate one room at a time, rather than needing a strategy for the entire space. However, it is important to bear in mind that where there are views from area to area, colours should not jar and patterns should not clash. The hall and stairs are important in this respect — intense colours or striking patterns here are likely to restrict your choice elsewhere.

In the past, the French sitting room was a formal salon, rather like the Victorian parlour. Now it is much more of a family room and a place to relax. The natural focal point is the fireplace, but it is also important to emphasize any connection with the outdoors if there is direct access to a terrace, balcony or garden.

With pressure on space, eating areas often have to be accommodated within another room — in the kitchen, living room or even in a large hallway. If possible, it is a good idea to make the most of outdoor views by setting up a dining area in a sunny corner, conservatory or even in the garden.

The kitchen is the heart of the home. The advent of the modern convenience kitchen with its appliances and fitted units poses a dilemma for devotees of this style. But rather than attempting to disguise the refrigerator, oven or dishwasher it is better to accept their presence and emphasize homely qualities with wooden surfaces, natural finishes, and displays of traditional kitchen paraphernalia which can look very attractive.

Bathrooms suffer from a similar problem, although there are more solutions. Modern fittings can be clad in painted panelling which minimizes their impact, or old fittings can be acquired from architectural salvage firms. Reproductions of traditional bathroom fittings are now widely available and are just as effective as the authentic pieces. Chairs, cupboards, towel rails and period accessories can also help to promote a furnished look which dispels the customary clinical image of most bathrooms.

Bedrooms can be treated like true retreats, decorated in restful colours and furnished very simply. For a period atmosphere, you can emphasize the bed with drapery, hangings or an exotic canopy.

Above All the elements of a country kitchen: hanging bunches of drying
herbs and flowers, a scrubbed dining table, a wooden dresser
with rows of preserves and a roaring fire in the open hearth —
a very traditional form of decoration.

Top A plain aquamarine screen and a vase of tulips repeat the colours of the
upholstery in a simple coordinated look, creating a sense of harmony without being
too rigid. *Above* Mint green and terracotta, the colours of the countryside,
are given equal weight in the decoration of this living room.

Top left Simplicity is often the most effective approach. Here, a painted white console
table provides room for a display of blue-and-white pottery which is
informal but uncluttered. **Above left** A trailing vine and flourishing greenery brings
the outdoors into a sunny living room.

Above *As well as being used as a way of creating a sense of intimacy and enclosure, pattern can also be displayed in a room. Here, a bold mantelpiece display of blue-and-white ceramics is matched in impact by a vivid quilted throw and some cushion covers.*

Below *Despite the presence of modern appliances,
this kitchen/dining area has been
decorated and furnished to avoid a clinical, modern
look — the emphasis is on natural elements.
The black-and-white tiled floor is a classic element of
the traditional French kitchen and it is extremely
practical. The plain wooden table and chairs together
with the jugs of daisies help to make a
sympathetic blend of old and new.* **Below right** *Eating
outdoors is one of the central pleasures of
French life. A blue-and-white checked cloth and a
canvas sunshade set the scene.*

Above left None of the comforts and convenience of the modern kitchen have been sacrificed, but the overall style is light and cheerful. Blue-and-white tiles inset into the top of the table match those on the wall; hanging baskets lend a country air. **Above right** Simple natural materials, displayed in the rush-bottomed chairs and quarry-tiled floor make an evocative setting for enjoying food. **Right** A table dressed for entertaining.

*Top This painted brass bedstead is piled with bolsters and cushions covered in rich, oriental fabrics. **Above left** A canopy of netting contrasts with the rustic, carved headboard and blue-washed walls. **Above right** A harmony of blue patterns; checks, spots and floral motifs.*

*Top Indigo curtains suspended from poles are the only decorative touch in this simple country bedroom. **Above left** The look of the past is easy to achieve in bathrooms by seeking out period fixtures and fittings. **Above right** A sink inset into a marble-topped dresser.*

Decorative arrangement is one of the most enjoyable and expressive aspects of this style. Although there is plenty of scope for surrounding yourself with personal treasures, curios and mementoes, displays can have a practical purpose as well: rows of preserves, open shelves of china and a gleaming line of copper-bottomed pans are all beautiful and useful.

There is, however, an art to arrangement. A successful display is neither a hodge-podge of everything you own (cluttering table tops and mantelpieces) nor is it a regimented row of knick-knacks. Small objects are best grouped informally to increase their impact; they can be related by colour, form or type, such as collections of coloured glass, enamelled boxes or blue-and-white pottery. The same principle can be applied to the hanging of pictures as well as to the arranging of flowers in a vase or plants on a plantstand. To avoid clutter and to give each display enough room to really work, it is not a good idea to put everything out on show at once. Displays have much more life if they are changed from time to time.

Objects need not be restricted to the simply beautiful. Artefacts with a practical past — antique

Above left A cascade of plants and flowers, including many geraniums, arranged so that each has the benefit of light while maintaining a decorative appearance.
Above right A sunny room is transformed into a conservatory overflowing with large bushy palms and trailing, climbing plants.

bird cages or old hand tools — together with everyday objects, such as kitchen utensils, bunches of drying herbs ·or earthenware casseroles, are worthy of as much attention as an oriental vase.

Cut flowers and potted plants of all varieties help to bring the outdoors in. Again, informality is important. The aim is to suggest the abundance of a country garden: cheerful and colourful mixtures are better than hot-house arrangements. You can group flowers by colour, coordinate near-shades or opt for riotous mixtures. In addition to more traditional varieties of flowers available from the florist, you can use branches of flowering blossom, so-called 'weeds' such as cow parsley and humble meadow flowers such as daisies and buttercups.

Ideally, arrange houseplants to make an indoor garden. It is better to group smaller plants together, if their needs allow, than to display them singly. Trailing, encroaching species such as ivy should be virtually allowed to take over in a sunny corner. Hanging baskets, a luxuriant fern in a *jardinière* or a tumbling collection of plants on a plantstand all exhibit the sheer density of foliage and a sense of movement, all important for a natural look. Foliage and greenery are good complements to natural fabrics: wood, coir, sisal and seagrass.

Above left *The same rules apply to flower arrangements as to displaying collections; group plants and containers together to maximize their impact and to create wonderful variety.* **Above right** *An antique cane hatstand makes an unusual support for ivy and other climbing species.*

Above A collection of glassware arranged on glass shelves makes a sparkling
display in this spectacular dining room. Candles cleverly arranged in a shallow glass
bowl make the most of the glittering, reflective table setting, transforming a
simple arrangement for a dinner-party.

Above *Curios, such as antique birdcages and old wooden toys, are just as much at home as rustic craftwork, such as baskets, hand-painted crockery and simple, glazed earthenware. There is always room for flowers of all kinds, especially those that suggest the country garden.*

INDEX

Figures in italics refer to photographs

ACKNOWLEDGMENTS

MMC = La Maison de Marie Claire

1 Jean-Paul Bonhommet; 2 MMC Nicolas/Postic; 4-5 MMC Godeaut/Belmont; 6 MMC Hussenot/Belmont; 7 above right MMC Primois/Belmont; 7 above left Arcaid/Richard Bryant; 8 MMC Girardeau/Comte; 10-11 Jean-Paul Bonhommet; 12 left MMC Chabaneix/Puech; 12 right Primois/Pellé; 13-14 Jean-Paul Bonhommet; 15 above left MMC Primois/Pellé; 15 centre left MMC Millet/Belmont; 15 below left MMC Coriat/Bayle; 15 above right MMC Coriat/Bayle; 15 centre right MMC Duronsoy; 15 below right Eric Crichton; 15 background photograph MMC Eriaud; 16 Jean-Paul Bonhommet; 17 left MMC Eriaud; 17 right MMC Scotto/Belmont; 18 MMC Mouries/Sabarros; 18-19 MMC Rozès/Hirsch-Marie; 19 MMC Mahé/Mahé; 20 MMC Chabaneix/Puech; 21 above MMC Sarramon/de Roquette; 21 below MMC Duronsoy/Phuong-Pfeufer; 22 MMC Chabaneix/Benard; 22-23 MMC Dirand/Hirsch-Marie; 23 MMC Mouries/Sabarros; 24 MMC Korniloff/Hirsch-Marie; 25 left MMC Girardeau/Postic; 25 centre MMC Scotto/Belmont; 25 right MMC Hussenot/Belmont; 26 MMC Nicolas/Postic; 27-28 MMC Sarramon/Forgeur; 29 left MMC Girardeau/Puech + Postic; 29 right MMC Pataut/Comte; 30 Jean-Paul Bonhommet; 31 above left MMC Pataut/Bayle; 31 below left MMC Girardeau/Postic + Puech; 31 right MMC Scotto/Belmont; 32 left MMC Hussenot/Belmont; 32 right MMC Hussenot/Puech; 32-33 MMC Godeaut/Belmont; 33 MMC Girardeau/Puech; 34-35 Jean-Paul Bonhommet; 36 above MMC Bayle/Pataut; 36 below MMC Duronsoy/Phuong-Pfeuffer; 36-37 MMC Nicolas/Postic; 37 MMC Godeaut/Belmont; 38 MMC Scotto/Belmont; 39 Christine Tiberghien; 40 left MMC Eriaud/Comte; 40 right MMC Pataut/Bayle; 40-41 Jean-Paul Bonhommet; 41 above left MMC Nicolas/Postic; 41 above right MMC Chabaneix/Bayle; 41 below MMC Godeaut/Belmont; 42 MMC Nicolas/Postic; 43 above MMC Mouries/Sabarros; 43 below Jean-Paul Bonhommet; 44 above MMC Chabaneix/Puech; 44 below Jean-Paul Bonhommet; 45 above MMC Chabaneix/Puech; 45 below Jean-Paul Bonhommet; 46 Jean-Paul Bonhommet; 47 above left MMC Chabaneix/Benard + Postic; 47 centre left MMC Pataut/Bayle; 47 below left MMC Hussenot/Belmont; 47 above right MMC Pataut/Bayle; 47 centre right Jean-Paul Bonhommet; 47 below right MMC Dugied + Millet/Belmont; 48-49 MMC Dirand/Chavel; 50 left MMC Korniloff/Comte; 50 right MMC Touillon/Lefebure; 51 Jean-Paul Bonhommet; 52 Tate Gallery, London; © DACS, 1988 53 above left MMC Pataut; 53 centre left Garden Picture Library/Ron Sutherland; 53 below left MMC Korniloff/Hourdin; 53 above right MMC Pataut/Belmont + Pascal; 53 centre right Jean-Paul Bonhommet; 53 below right MMC Sarramon/Forgeur; 54 Jean-Paul Bonhommet; 55 above left MMC Chabaneix/Rozensztroch; 55 above right MMC Pataut/Comte; 55 below MMC Korniloff/Chauvel; 56 Jean-Paul Bonhommet; 57 above MMC Dirand + Rozès; 57 below Jean-Paul Bonhommet; 58 above left MMC Pataut/Comte; 58 above right MMC Guy Bouchet; 58 below MMC Sarramon/Forgeur; 59 left MMC Chabaneix/Puech; 59 right Jean-Paul Bonhommet; 60 Jean-Paul Bonhommet; 61 MMC Chabaneix/Postic; 62 above MMC Pataut/Bayle; 62 below MMC Pataut/Comte; 63 above left MMC Pataut/Bayle; 63 above right MMC Scotto/Belmont; 63 below MMC Girardeau/Postic; 64 MMC Scotto/Postic; 64-65 Jean-Paul Bonhommet; 65 left MMC Touillon/Lefebure; 65 right Jean-Paul Bonhommet; 66 left MMC Nicolas/Postic; 66 above right MMC Dirand/Berkier + Chauvel; 66 below right MMC Nicolas/Postic; 67 above left MMC Hussenot/Puech; 67 below left MMC Nicolas/Postic; 67 above right MMC Girardeau/Phuong-Pfeuffer; 67 below right MMC

Nicolas/Postic; 68 above MMC Touillon/Lefebure; 68 below Jean-Paul Bonhommet; 69 Jean-Paul Bonhommet; 70 above Jean-Paul Bonhommet; 70 below MMC Girardeau/Postic + Comte + Hirsch-Marie; 70-71 Jean-Paul Bonhommet; 71 MMC Pataut/Ardouin; 72 above left MMC Korniloff/Hirsch-Marie; 72 below left MMC Primois/Olry; 72 right MMC Pataut/Bayle; 73 Jean-Paul Bonhommet; 74 left Jean-Paul Bonhommet; 74 right MMC Mouries/Sabarros; 74-75 Jean-Paul Bonhommet; 75 above MMC Pataut/Puech; 75 below Jean-Paul Bonhommet; 76-77 Jean-Paul Bonhommet; 78 above MMC Chabaneix; 78 below MMC Sarramon/Forgeur; 79 above MMC Chabaneix/Puech; 79 below MMC Hussenot; 80-81 MMC Pataut/Puech; 82 left Jean-Paul Bonhommet; 82 right MMC Pataut/Bayle; 83 Jean-Paul Bonhommet; 84 above MMC Duronsoy/Laroze; 84 below Jean-Paul Bonhommet; 85 above MMC Touillon/Lefebure; 85 below Jean-Paul Bonhommet; 86 MMC Chabaneix; 87 above left MMC Chabaneix; 87 centre left MMC Chabaneix/Rozensztroch; 87 below left MMC Pataut/Bayle; 87 above and right Jean-Paul Bonhommet; 87 below right MMC Hussenot/Belmont; 88-89 Jean-Paul Bonhommet; 90 left Jean-Paul Bonhommet; 90 right MMC Primois/Belmont; 91 Jean-Paul Bonhommet; 92 MMC Chabaneix/Bernard; 93 above left MMC Primois/Pellé; 93 below left MMC Sarramon; 93 above right MMC Pataut; 93 centre right MMC Primois/Pellé; 93 below right MMC Pataut/Bayle; 93 background MMC Mounicq/Vallery-Radot; 94 MMC Bouchet/Pellé; 95 above left MMC Godeaut/Belmont; 95 below left MMC Maclean/Mahé; 95 right MMC Mouries/Sabarros; 96 MMC Pataut/Bayle + Berthier; 97 MMC Sarramon/de Roquette; 98 MMC Rozès/Hirsch-Marie; 98-99 Jean-Paul Bonhommet; 99 above MMC Sarramon/de Roquette; 99 below Jean-Paul Bonhommet; 100 left Jean-Paul Bonhommet; 100 right MMC Rozès/Hirsch-Marie; 101 Jean-Paul Bonhommet; 102 left Jean-Paul Bonhommet; 102 above right MMC Sarramon/de Roquette; 102 below right MMC Mouries/Sabarros; 103 above left MMC Sarramon/de Roquette; 103 below left MMC Chabaneix/Ardouin; 103 right MMC Chabaneix/Puech; 104 above left MMC Sarramon/Forgeur; 105 above MMC Eriaud/Comte; 105 below left MMC Mouries/Sabarros; 105 below right MMC Mouries/Sabarros; 106-107 Jean-Paul Bonhommet; 108 left MMC Rozès/Hirsch-Marie; 108 right MMC Mouries/Sabarros; 109 above MMC Pataut/Lautier; 109 below MMC Korniloff/Hirsch-Marie; 110-111 MMC Sarramon/de Roquette; 111 MMC Rozès/Hirsch-Marie; 112 MMC Pataut/Puech; 113 above MMC Chabaneix/Mahé; 113 below MMC Mouries/Sabarros; 114 above MMC Hussenot/Puech; 114 below MMC Pataut/Bayle; 114-117 Jean-Paul Bonhommet; 118 left Jean-Paul Bonhommet; 118 right MMC Hussenot/Charras; 118-119 Jean-Paul Bonhommet; 119 above Jean-Paul Bonhommet; 119 below MMC Hussenot/Puech; 120 above MMC Rozès/Hirsch-Marie; 120 below left MMC Sarramon/de Roquette; 120 below right MMC Chabaneix/Puech; 121 above MMC Duronsoy/Hourdin; 121 below left MMC Rozès/Hirsch-Marie; 121 below right MMC Hussenot/Belmont; 122 left MMC Rozès/Hirsch-Marie; 122 right MMC Chabaneix/Viane; 123 left Jean-Paul Bonhommet; 123 right MMC Hussenot/Belmont; 124 MMC Chabaneix/Bayle; 125 above and centre left MMC Chabaneix/Bernard; 125 below left MMC Pataut/Bayle; 125 above right MMC Primois/Belmont; 125 centre right MMC Sarramon/de Roquette; 125 below right MMC Pataut.